Mindfulness V

Discover Peace and Free
Anxiety and Worry By Learning How to Live
Mindfully in The Present

By Nathan Weaver

© **Copyright 2019 - All rights reserved.**

The content contained within this book may not be reproduced, duplicated or transmitted without direct written permission from the author or the publisher.

Under no circumstances will any blame or legal responsibility be held against the publisher or author for any damages, reparation, or monetary loss due to the information contained within this book. Either directly or indirectly.

Legal Notice:

This book is copyright protected. This book is only for personal use. You cannot amend, distribute, sell, use, quote or paraphrase any part, or the content within this book, without the consent of the author or publisher.

Disclaimer Notice:

Please note the information contained within this document is for educational and entertainment purposes only. All effort has been executed to present accurate, up to date and reliable, complete information. No warranties of any kind are declared or implied. Readers acknowledge that the author is not engaging in the rendering of legal, financial, medical or professional advice. The content within this book has been derived from various sources. Please consult a licensed professional before attempting any techniques outlined in this book.

By reading this document, the reader agrees that under no

circumstances is the author responsible for any losses, direct or indirect, which are incurred as a result of the use of information contained within this document, including, but not limited to, —errors, omissions, or inaccuracies.

Table of Contents

Introduction 1
Chapter 1: Explaining Mindfulness 5
    Mindfulness in Everyday Life 8
Chapter 2: How to Begin Being Mindful 12
    Step 1: Breathing 13
    Step 2: Senses 14
    Step 3: Body Scan 15
    Step 4: Concentrate On Breathing 17
    Step 5: Allow Your Mind to Wander 18
    Tips for Fast Improvement 19
Chapter 3: Intro to Cognitive Restructuring 22
    A Short Primer on CBT 22
    Techniques Used in CBT 26
Chapter 4: Using Cognitive Restructuring in Real Life ... 30
    Fear Setting 31
    Get Rid of the Fear and Date Anyone 37
Chapter 5: Stress and Flow State 41
    Chronic Stress 44
    Positive Stress 47
    Delving Into Hidden Powers 50
Chapter 6: Why You Should Consider Visualizing 55
    Embodied Cognition 56
    Visualization 58
Chapter 7: Why is Belief so Powerful? 60

Becoming Socially Fearless..61
The Law of Attraction..64
Conclusion 66

Thank you for buying this book and I hope that you will find it useful. If you will want to share your thoughts on this book, you can do so by leaving a review on the [Amazon page](), it helps me out a lot.

Introduction

In case there is one skill which you could study which would make each and every area of your life nicer, what would it be?

Certainly, it would be the capability to manage your feelings and to manage how you think.

This might seem like an unusual claim, but the capability to manage your feelings and how you react to a scenario is not only the key to happiness but likewise the trick to being able to obtain whatever you desire from life.

Why? Due to the fact that it's our interpretation of occasions, more than the occasions themselves, that determine our joy, emotional state and performance. Not just that, but our feelings and the neurotransmitters which manage them are what changes our ability to concentrate, to recall information and to be inventive.

Let's picture a situation where you're trapped within a lorry which has flipped over and is now looming the edge of a cliff. The tiniest movement might ruin the balance and send you falling to your death.

What occurs to you in this scenario? You freeze, obviously, but simultaneously, your body ends up being *really* engaged. Your brain understands you're in harm, and therefore it causes particular neurons in mind to fire and produce neurotransmitters. These neurotransmitters include those such as cortisol, dopamine, and norepinephrine.

At the same time, the sympathetic nervous system reacts to these signs and starts creating more chemicals of its own. Specifically, a portion called the adrenal medulla is going to produce noradrenaline and adrenaline and this is going to lead to various physiological alterations in your body: your heart rate rises, your muscles contract and your brain speeds up.

But here's the twist: it appears that a rescue team has been working unbeknownst to you and has connected the lorry to the solid ground by a chain. You're entirely safe.

The response of your body is in response to your view and your perspective and not the reality.

And as we are going to see within this guide, there are plenty of situations where we think we're in more harm than we truly are leading to the stress reaction. And as we'll likewise see, that stress reaction is capable of triggering all sorts of mental and health issues.

If you can obtain control of your emotional reaction, then, you may stop that stressful reaction and alternatively remain cool and focused.

But the power of managing your emotions is a lot deeper than that. As we are going to see eventually in this guide, the capability to boost your self-confidence could actually result in all sorts of adjustments in your life which lead to you being more effective, more prosperous, even wealthier.

And it doesn't end there! Managing your emotions also implies you'll have the ability to conquer stressful situations and even fears! Bid farewell to a fear of public speaking . And also, regulating your emotions could aid you to prevent arguments and shouting matches in your relationship-- which is going to lead to more unified and joyful home life.

Then there are the ways that your feelings could make you more dynamic and more effective. Did you know, for example, that you could boost muscle fiber employment and possibly delve into superhuman strength by entering the right mood? Did you know that the appropriate mix of neurochemistry could give you great recall?

This guide will present you how to take advantage of all those things and simultaneously, it is going to show you how you can basically get a bit of quiet and peace by soothing your brain and taking a break. Read on and prepare yourself to change your life.

Chapter 1: Explaining Mindfulness

I could organize this guide in such a manner that you will need to build up to mindfulness. I could discuss how horrible for you stress is, or I could discuss neuroscience.

But I'll come to that later. What you most likely wish to know right off the bat is simply what mindfulness is. Where did it originate from? And how could you utilize it just to get a bit calmer and comfortable in your life?

We'll take a look at that initially and from there, we'll look into how you could use some more technical neuroscience so as to delve into the more extensive capabilities of your brain.

So what precisely is mindfulness? Basically, mindfulness is a kind of meditation which has been embraced by CBT. CBT, consequently, is 'cognitive behavioral therapy'; a psychotherapeutic process which could be utilized to address all sorts of psychological problems such as anxiety, fears, addiction, and so on.

Mindfulness basically provides us a tool which we could utilize to not only soothe our thoughts and get away from the stressors of the day but also review the contents of our mind with the goal of self-improvement.

Meditation typically has something of a 'bad' image. That is to say that a bunch of folks connect it with religion or esoteric concepts and they believe that they simply cannot meditate unless they're' spiritual'. This could be off-putting for somebody who doesn't keep any religious ideas or who doesn't like mystical concepts as a whole.

But as a matter of fact, you could engage in meditation no matter if you are religious or an atheist. All meditation truly is, is a guided effort to regulate your thoughts and the content of your mind and thus to gain some calmness and quiet or at minimum to be ready to comprehend the contents of your own brain better.

Often this implies entirely muting all thoughts. Many kinds of meditation, like transcendental meditation, advise you to think of 'completely nothing' and frequently this is accomplished by concentrating on your breathing, a mantra or a physical item such as a candle flame. This could be tough for novices, as they regularly find their mind straying.

The strategy behind mindfulness meditation then is not to attempt and unload your thoughts but rather to just step back from them and 'monitor' them like a separated third party. By doing this, you aren't allowing your thoughts influence you and make you worried but you likewise aren't going to deal with not being 'permitted' to think anything.

At the same time, utilizing this technique is going to likewise enable you to end up being more aware of your own feelings and thus able to modify any thoughts which are leading you into problems. For example, if you regularly find yourself considering how you might harm yourself, you might observe that this is a bad habit and after that try to mend that.

This might be the long-term objective of mindfulness when utilized in CBT. In the short-term, however, we are merely to utilize it so as to extract ourselves from our feelings and emotions to ensure that we can get a bit of tranquility and therefore recover prepared to take on the day ahead.

Mindfulness in Everyday Life

This is what mindfulness describes in many cases but it has likewise been appropriated to suggest a great deal more. If mindfulness means being more familiar with your thoughts, then it could likewise be used outside of meditation and to how you deal with your day. In this instance, mindfulness merely means being conscious of what you're concentrating on and what you're feeling at any given point. This works due to the fact that very frequently you'll find that your mind isn't possibly where it ought to be.

For instance, if you are going through a lovely scenic woodland, however, you are thinking of work, then as far as your body is involved, you might as well be at your job. In this situation, mindfulness could be utilized just to make yourself more knowledgeable about where you are and to, in fact, pay attention to what's around you. That implies feeling the wind on your skin, checking out the lovely flowers and smelling the clean air. When you perform all that, you are going to gain a lot more from the experience.

Also, you could use mindfulness to guide your awareness to all sorts of other things. For instance, your physical sensations. Frequently we aren't familiar with simply how we're sitting or how we're standing.

Take a minute now to reflect on this. How relaxed are you at the minute? Does any area of your body hurt? In case you're sitting, then where is the majority of pressure on you? Can you sense your clothes against your body? A watch, perhaps? How cozy are you?

This sort of mindfulness could be beneficial if you wish to attempt and remedy your posture but also if you wish to enhance your capabilities in sports or just to obtain more success.

Being more mindful of how you talk can at the same time aid you to speak more smoothly, to stop utilizing demeaning words, to stop cussing, or to alter the entire way how folks view you. For instance, if you wish to sound more educated, then you could just attempt utilizing bigger words or talking a tad more slowly.

You could likewise utilize mindfulness to be more satisfied in day-to-day life. Just try to stop allowing negative feelings to impact you by identifying them as momentary and troublesome. You can just 'observe' that you're getting angry and recognize that your feelings are going to be polluted by that. With practice, this could make you a lot more relaxed and much healthier individual.

But what do you discover when you make an effort and do this? In all probability, you'll discover that you forget. This is just the same way that you fail to remember to get bread whenever your partner asks you to. And it's just the same way you fail to remember to grab your keys while exiting the house.

The point is, the majority of the time we have no authority over what we're concentrated on or what we're focusing on. And because of this, we find ourselves overlooking things, embracing bad habits or worrying when we ought to be enjoying ourselves.

Practicing mindfulness both as a type of meditation and throughout the day can, as a result, aid you to enhance your ability to regulate your thoughts and therefore to choose how you wish to strengthen yourself and what you wish to focus on.

Chapter 2: How to Begin Being Mindful

So that's mindfulness essentially, the following question is how you start applying it.

One possibility is to utilize online 'guided meditations.' These are basically audios that direct you on what to do as you attempt meditating. For instance, they may inform you to shut your eyes and breathe in and out throughout the nose.

Then they could inform you to contemplate your body. One especially good resource that accomplishes this is the Headspace App that could be downloaded for iOS or Android but that is likewise available to utilize via the web. This is going to talk you through various directed meditations, but only the initial ten are cost-free. Still, you could discover enough from those ten sessions to then flourish without the app.

In general, though, the majority of mindfulness meditations are going to take a very identical method and you could undergo the steps then without essentially having to be talked through it.

And as a matter of fact, if you *are able to* do your meditation without instruction, then you ought to find that you're in fact more successful at it due to the fact that you won't be constantly interrupted by somebody's voice.

Let's discuss what the steps are going to typically be for a mindfulness meditation program.

Step 1: Breathing

The primary thing to do is to begin breathing. You may do this utilizing something referred to as 'equal breathing' from yoga. Here, you inhale through the nose and exhale through the mouth. As you accomplish this, you retain every inhalation and exhalation for 3 seconds. These lengthy draws in and lengthy exhalations are going to enable you to entirely fill up the lungs with clean oxygen and eliminate all the CO_2.

But to be truthful, you could utilize any sort of breathing so long as it is gradual, intentional and full. The direction they give on the Headspace App, for example, is just to 'breathe loud enough so that the individual beside you would manage to hear.'

Why breathing? Basically, breathing gradually is the ideal way to signal to the body that the coast is clear and you're secure. We breathe rapidly when we're worried to get more air around our bodies and we can inhale more slowly when we are calm. Therefore, breathing deeply and gradually is going to aid us to leave the 'fight or flight' state and to enter the 'rest and digest' state alternatively. This ought to correct our heart rate variance, decrease cortisol and get us prepared to go into a relaxed state.

Step 2: Senses

Next, you are frequently told to pay attention to your physical senses. This implies observing the sounds, smells, and also the temperature throughout the room. Your eyes are going to typically be closed, so sight is dismissed from this one.

The goal here is not to 'search' for sounds or attempt to hear them. Rather, just observe the sounds which you don't typically. You may discover that you are able to hear squeaking in the house, perhaps you are able to hear the next-door neighbors, perhaps you could hear the rain outdoors or the wind. There are possibly far off birds and/or traffic.

This is often a great instance of just how little we typically focus on and how much richer our experience ends up being when we engage in mindfulness. It's likewise a fantastic way to get involved in that habit and to begin unwinding the body even further.

Step 3: Body Scan

Body scan meditation is in some cases referred to as being its own thing, but it could be utilized as a component of any meditation session. The concept here is just to become more mindful of your own body as we explained earlier but to accomplish this by methodically starting on top of the head and after that moving progressively through to the toes, observing how you feel at every stage.

If you wish to utilize this procedure to get to sleep, at that point, it could be a fantastic tool for that objective as well. The ideal way to accomplish this, though, is to make an effort to completely relax the muscles by initially contracting and then releasing every portion of your body as you go through it. What you'll discover is that you hold big amounts of tension all over from your face muscles, to your neck, to your limbs. Once you acknowledge this and let it go, you are going to feel much more relaxed and ultimately, which could allow you to enter restful and deep sleep.

In the meantime, though, we're just examining the body and utilizing this as a method to end up being more mindful of our own selves and to start the procedure of introspection and self-directed attention.

Step 4: Concentrate On Breathing

After observing every part of the body, go back to the chest and pay specific focus to the way it fluctuates. As you accomplish this, you can likewise take this chance to correct your breathing.

Odds are, that when you initially observe your own breathing, you'll discover that you are breathing in so that your chest broadens initially. But actually, it ought to be your abdomen which moves initially and this ought to after that be followed by your chest. Appropriate breathing (called abdominal breathing) ought to begin by enabling the stomach to loosen up and stick out and then filling the lungs.

This is helpful since the process creates space in your abdominal cavity. This at that point, enables the lungs to expand into that space, and that is after that followed by them extending upwards through your chest too.

This kind of breathing permits you to ingest more oxygen and to, thus, activate even more pleasure hormones. The majority of us don't utilize this type of breathing though due to the fact that we have hunched postures that tuck our stomach and hinder us from managing to breathe from there. The outcome is that we wind up breathing with a lot shallower and quicker breaths, that in fact raises cortisol and stress.

But don't stress over that if you don't wish to. In the meantime, just observe your own breath and take this chance to count your breaths as they come in and out. This is the portion which will function a bit like transcendental meditation by silencing a great deal of the activity across the brain.

Step 5: Allow Your Mind to Wander

Once you've accomplished this for a little while and you're feeling especially calm, it's time just to free your mind and allow it to do whatever it desires. Now your goal is not to attempt and silence or control your thoughts. Rather, you just let your mind stray naturally or to remain entirely still if it wishes to.

The explanation that is frequently utilized is that you're 'monitoring thoughts proceed like clouds'. Headspace defines your thoughts in these instances as being more like cars in the street. It highlights the importance of viewing the 'cars' pass by but not going out into the road to go after the traffic. This is all about detached monitoring.

After you have accomplished this for some time, you could just allow your thoughts to slowly go back to normal and lightly open your eyes.

Tips for Fast Improvement

A great deal of folks attempt to begin meditating, but they wind up falling short. Why is this?

One issue is that a lot of us wish to get instant results and want to feel immediately different. When this doesn't occur, we wind up annoyed and stressed. This is the nastiest mindset you could perhaps take to mindfulness meditation. The entire point is that you are to allow your mind do anything it desires. As soon as you begin pushing it in one direction or another, you are going to drop that all-important freedom and begin generating stress hormones.

Also, attempt not to get too disturbed with yourself if you attempt this and your brain keeps straying or you keep getting sidetracked. If you become itchy, it's okay to scratch your skin. If you require a glass of water, stand up and get one. Don't attempt and pressure anything; simply allow yourself to 'be' as you are truly.

If you truly want assistance jump-starting your progress though, at that point, you ought to think about 'priming' yourself. Priming is a terminology utilized in psychology which just pertains to prepping the brain in a particular way.

In some cases, that means affecting the responses we provide to questions by presenting a certain stimulus. But in other instances, it means altering our emotions. In this instance, it pays to perform anything calming, but that, nonetheless, calls for concentration just before you attempt meditating.

So, for instance, you could attempt relaxing in a lovely but novel location. Novel scenery boost hormones and neurotransmitters connected with concentration, while being in natural surroundings has been demonstrated to make us more loosened up and to stimulate slower brainwaves.

Lastly, don't be too aggressive relative to how frequently you plan to meditate. Another traditional error is to set out with the plan that you will meditate for 30 minutes each day. This is doomed to for fail unless you presently devoting 30 minutes of each day bored out of your head. Begin with something modest-- even just 5 minutes prior to waking up and afterward, you could improve this habit.

Chapter 3: Intro to Cognitive Restructuring

Mindfulness and cognitive restructuring fit like cheese and chutney. In CBT, mindfulness is typically utilized together with cognitive restructuring to the point that they are indivisible.

Utilizing mindfulness meditation and mindfulness in awake life will assist you in discovering how to step back from your feelings and with time, you'll discover that you end up being calmer, more concentrated and healthier.

But it could be utilized for a great deal more once you acknowledge the strength this tool has for creating change. The point is that when you recognize negative thoughts which are detrimentally impacting your life, you can now transform them. And that's where cognitive restructuring shows up.

A Short Primer on CBT

CBT is right now the most prominent choice for dealing with mental illness among the majority of big health organizations. The approach was presented fairly recently and is an organic extension of another institution of psychology which reigned in the past (around the 50s).

That institution was 'behaviorism' and was completely described by the idea of conditioning and association. The concept was that in case you experienced two stimuli simultaneously frequently enough, they would ultimately end up being linked in your head.

Today we understand this to be correct: in neuroplasticity 'neurons which fire together, wire together'. This implies that if two neurons activate at the identical moment frequently enough, they eventually develop a very solid connection that might cause the other to fire unwillingly.

This was shown famously by Ivan Pavlov who practiced with on dogs. He rang a bell any time he fed the canine attendees and gradually, this developed an association by means of 'positive reinforcement'. Eventually, this resulted in the dogs drooling whenever the bell was sounded. As far as their minds were involved, bell equaled food.

This identical idea was after that applied to human psychology. The theory was that we might learn fears, for instance, by associating unfavorable experiences with benign objects. Also, it was supposed that you could manage a fear via 'reassociation.' In case you make sure that somebody associates that input with favorable things again, they ultimately lose the fear. And this technique proved effective in various studies.

Behaviorism went a bit too far, it declared that each aspect of the human journey was learned in this manner. We found out how to gesture since when we grabbed things as kids, folks passed them to us. We understood to walk since we kept tipping over when we did it incorrectly Etc.

Whatever we did then was thought to be completely encouraged by the reward centers of our mind, which consequently helped us create fresh associations and establish new behaviors. The things we didn't find out ourselves directly, we could learn 'vicariously' via social conditioning, observing others for instance.

For many years this idea ruled supreme but ultimately, it began to lose favor as it was powerless to clarify every element of our psychology. Eventually, it became evident that there has to be an additional 'interior' aspect and this is where the 'cognitive' aspect appears. Cognitive behavioral therapy then takes behavioralism and employs the concept that you could likewise strengthen experiences, both good and bad, by contemplating them.

For example, you could learn to be scared of heights even when you've never slipped from a height. How? By continuously considering how unpleasant it could be to fall from a height. Simply put, if you keep visualizing that falling has to be harmful and if you say to yourself things such as 'those railings don't appear safe', then you can induce yourself to be scared.

What's more, is that every time you think something such as this and then avoid the height as a consequence, you are basically strengthening that belief as if you had fallen.

So the concept behind CBT is to utilize the fundamentals of behaviorism but to integrate these with the cognitive element. That implies not just utilizing elements such as 'reassociation' yet likewise 'thinking' cures.

Techniques Used in CBT

So one instance of this is to utilize mindfulness meditation. Just by deciding not to allow your thoughts and feelings impact you, you can end up being less managed by them and consequently less prone to your own ruminations and worries.

But there are a lot more facets to this too and these have a tendency to fall under the heading of 'cognitive restructuring' or simply put-- altering your thoughts.

One instance is a thing referred to as 'thought challenging.' Here, you just break down one of your thoughts or theories and thereby evaluate just how precise it is. For example, you could find that you are scared of public speaking since you believe folks are going to giggle at you if you stutter. This is a devastating belief that is actually making you far more prone to stuttering.

So what you have to do if you want to conquer this is to look at the notion and ask: is it reasonable? What you are going to discover 95% of the time is that this idea is improbable and misguided. The majority of people would not be cruel enough to make fun of you if you stuttered and even if they did, it wouldn't make a difference since you wouldn't see them again.

Maybe you could feel lame in case you stutter and folks laugh. Once again, you ought to evaluate that: having the ability to chat confidently; however, it comes out and not worry about the result is, in fact, an indication that you're quite self-assured and unconcerned!

I, in fact, utilized this method myself when I had a phobia. I used to come with a somewhat unpleasant phobia of peeing in public urinals. My worry was that if I couldn't go, at that point individuals would look at me and assume I was unusual for mingling there and 'not actually doing anything.'

Then I recognized that the majority of the time I was in that scenario, I was in the bar. Simply put? The majority of the other people in the toilets were most likely drunk and unaware of what I was doing! On the other hand, why did it matter what they believed anyway? Allow them to believe that! Ultimately, this helped me to conquer the phobia entirely, and now I have no issue whatsoever with it.

One more instance is one which combines the suggestions from CBT with more conventional ideas from behaviorism. This one is referred to as 'hypothesis testing.' Basically, it implies that you're evaluating your theory to figure out if it truly holds up.

So if you're scared folks are going to laugh if you stutter throughout public speaking, that implies you have to stutter on stage and allow everybody to see it intentionally. This is going to then consequently show you what occurs in that situation and what you are going to probably discover is that nothing at all happens. Individuals are kind and they are going to simply await you to wrap up and begin again.

Once more, I employed this in the real world. Except I really had no say in it this time. I was learning to drive and I kept delaying any time the lights turned green and I was at the front. Naturally, this occurred because of nerves: I was concerned that if I didn't leave faster off the mark, at that point, the traffic behind me would get upset and it would be extremely awkward.

So my driving instructor, being kind of rebelious, chose to slam on my handbrake and told me that we were going to sit there for the whole time that the light was green. Traffic behind me beeped their horns, folks yelled, but not a thing occurred. And after that, I started just okay the following moment it turned green.

Chapter 4: Using Cognitive Restructuring in Real Life

So now you understand how to utilize mindfulness and you understand how to utilize cognitive restructuring. Ideally, you've also managed to presume how the two could be linked: we use mindfulness to recognize the negative thoughts, and after that, we use cognitive restructuring so as to alter them.

This has been utilized for some time now to treat things such as fears, anxiety disorders, dependencies and a lot more.

But what if you don't possess any of those issues and you're entirely okay? Well, in that case, we can still utilize cognitive restructuring. Since the thing is, you can really utilize cognitive restructuring to enhance elements of your mind which aren't 'damaged'. Simply put, this isn't simply a method for healing but also a method for self-improvement. And there are numerous methods to utilize it to make yourself more relaxed, more positive and more productive.

Also, there are lots of things which resemble cognitive restructuring but don't actually fall under the identical heading.

We'll be revisiting this idea more in future but for now, let's check out some alternative ways to manage your thought patterns and some different motives for doing it.

Fear Setting

Frequently we think of anxiety and fear as being temporary reactions to circumstances or provocations. But actually, our anxiety and fear could be much longer-term and impact our choices, goal setting and judgments.

Tim Ferriss offers a principle referred to as 'fear setting' in The Four Hour Workweek as a method you could utilize to conquer your fears and therefore begin obtaining what you desire out of life. Let's say you're thinking about finding a new job, making a career change so you can go traveling, or launching your very own business.

You've been considering undertaking these things for a long while but the issue is that you're too scared to do it since you think you are going to wind up without work or without a loved one. Certainly, if you leave your existing job to go traveling, you wouldn't manage to get a job when you get back? And the longer you're jobless, the more unemployable you are going to end up being.

Ultimately, your partner will end up being sick and tired of subsisting due to a foolish decision you made and they'll go away. Then your home is going to be repossessed. And after that, you are going to wind up without a roof and alone.

That could all seem very over-the-top however this is the sort of thing we really think on a subconscious level at all times. And the reason we assume it is that people are naturally quite risk-averse. We developed in the wilderness where 'risk' would typically imply tigers. Because of this, we learned to become more reactive to risk and to protect our possessions more than we go after new resources.

But these days risk is quite rarely something life-threatening. Probably, risk is going to imply 'getting yelled at' but we blow it out of proportion since we're risk-averse individuals.

By now, you ought to ideally have the ability to guess what's following: though difficult, We will take these fears and beliefs and test them by checking out just how sensible they are. And Tim Ferriss' method is ideal for this.

So initially, consider what it is you wish to do and why you wish to do it. Now consider all the things that are currently holding you back from starting and trying. If we're referring to a career break, then your list of concerns and explanations might appear like this:

Presently's not a great time, you don't have a lot cash

You don't wish to leave your partner for so long

You're scared your job won't be there as soon as you return

You're scared you won't manage to find subsequent work

You're worried that you may eventually wind up penniless, in the red or homeless

Now let's evaluate each of these ideas. To accomplish that, we're looking not just at how probable they are but likewise how you'd manage if they were to transpire. Think of backups and things you might do to hinder them from being probable.

Presently's not a great time, you don't have a lot of money

o There's never really a great time, and if you travel intelligently you don't require much cash

o You might do the job online while you travel

o You really won't require that much cash

o Now is likely better than later

You don't wish to leave your partner for that much

o They very likely don't mind

o If it is crucial to you, then it's something you need to carry out

o It's advantageous to feeling spiteful toward your partner since they kept you from experiencing the world

You're scared your job won't be there as soon as you return

o It likely is going to be, go over it with your boss.

o Do you enjoy your work that much?

You're scared you won't manage to find subsequent work

o This is very improbable. If you're competent then travel is going to just contribute to your CV o You might even discover a new job and accept to begin later on

o If required, then you can get some part-time work or launch a side business

You're worried that you may eventually wind up penniless, in the red or homeless

o You can survive on savings a very long time

o You can make money in additional ways

o You likely have parents or buddies who would certainly take you in long before you went without a roof over your head

Now consider the alternative: do you wish never to go traveling? Do you wish to spend each single day stuck in that workplace without ever achieving the goals you wish to achieve? Let this inspire you more than the worry and now decide to break the ice.

The identical method could aid you to decide to begin a new career, to relocate to another country, or to undertake all the numerous other matters that you've been longing for.

Get Rid of the Fear and Date Anyone

So, in this instance, we've utilized thought challenging once more to break down our worries so that we are able to pursue whatever we desire in life.

However, one more technique you could utilize is to recognize those fears as legitimate but simply discover a strategy which reduces the risk. In this part, we'll check out a technique you can utilize for dating which is going to certainly give you the self-assurance to approach and date any person.

So let's suggest that you're the typical awkward dude, for argument's sake. You visit bars routinely with friends wishing to 'pull' but you're too scared to move toward the people on the dance floor. Why? Due to the fact that you're concerned they'll decline you and you are going to thus wind up feeling extremely awkward. That's a legitimate concern (even though we could question why it matters) so it's tough to refute it.

The easy answer? Reduce the risk and remove your possibility of failing.

To perform this, you could just evaluate the scenario before you approach anybody. So hang back far from the bar and chat with buddies. As you do, just check out the place for folks you're curious about and if you spot somebody, smile at them with eye contact. If they're intrigued, then you can guarantee they're going to smile in return. If they're definitely not interested? They'll likely just avert their gaze, and you are going to know about it. But in both situations, you haven't lost face, and you could continue to hold your head high. There's very little to be scared of.

If they've smiled, however, then you could most likely relatively easily approach them. That doesn't indicate they're automatically into you, however, it implies they at a minimum are available to the idea of chatting with you. So the following action is to go with your group of buddies to speak with their group of friends. Don't talk to them only; talk to the entire group so you simply appear as somebody welcoming, outgoing and captivating. Also, allow your friends mingle with their friends as well. When you get a minute, attempt to spend a little bit more time talking with the individual you were originally curious about and who offered you the go-ahead to come over.

If the chat is going properly with the individual you have an interest in, at that point, you could step it up one more degree by just offering to purchase them a drink. This is a very obvious sign that you're interested in them and so they likely won't say yes if they're interested in return. Now they're elsewhere. You can chat with them by themselves and evaluate the situation.

Lastly, ask if they wish to dance. And in case they say yes, utilize the identical approach: dance increasingly more closely up until ultimately, you're totally sure it's fine to make a move.

In this scenario, you have now moved toward somebody attractive in a bar, but at no moment is there any risk of rejection. If they don't wish to speak with you, they won't smile. In case they aren't engaged when you drop in, they'll create excuses and you can chat with their friends. If they change their minds, they can deny the drink. If you're sending out the inappropriate signals, then they are able to deny the dance. But at no point have you humiliated yourself and you haven't carried out anything that you can't 'recover' from.

Consider other things which you're scared to undertake in your life, evaluate why it is you're scared, and then imagine methods to navigate around that fear by staying clear of the worst-case scenarios!

Chapter 5: Stress and Flow State

We're just midway through the guide and already you should have picked up some rather valuable skills. You now understand how to go into a mindful state at any given opportunity to better enjoy your environment or at minimum just to get away from stress for a few moments of reprieve.

But let's rewind and check out that stress in a bit more detail. What is it regarding stress that renders it so severe? Why are we attempting to fight stress? And is stress always harmful?

In fact, stress is one thing which is completely misjudged by plenty of folks. Stress is not actually 'one thing'; instead, it is a spectrum of reactions that happen in reaction to harmful situations. Basically, when you spot a threat, your body reacts by discharging neurotransmitters and hormones which set off the 'fight or flight' reaction. This is the reaction that I explained earlier and it is regulated by the following neurotransmitters/hormones (neurotransmitters resemble hormones, but they impact the brain more immediately and don't endure as long):

Epinephrine.

Dopamine.

Serotonin.

Norepinephrine.

Glutamate.

Cortisol.

Estrogen.

Testosterone.

These then collectively induce a variety of symptoms which you ought to recognize if ever you've gotten involved in an argument, fight or unsafe situation.

These symptoms involve:

Feeling of dread.

Racing considerations.

Trembling.

Muscle contractions.

Vasodilation (expanding of the veins).

Raised heart rate.

Pupil dilation.

Resistance to pain.

Reduction of the immune system and gastrointestinal system so that more blood and materials could be delivered to the muscles and brain.

Raised sensitivity to sounds and illumination.

Shortsightedness.

Fast breathing.

Sweating.

Raised blood thickness to promote the blood to clot just in case of an injury.

Simply put, our body enters into a 'high-performance mode' by redirecting energy and supplies far from upkeep tasks and less immediately critical procedures. Our speed, strength, and capability to fight or climb rise and this helps make us more potent and more capable of taking action.

This reaction evolved in the wilderness to serve to aid us defend ourselves in the event of danger. If we noticed a predator, or if we found a forest fire, then these adjustments would enable us to escape. Similarly, we would end up being superior fighters when contending with members of our own species for materials.

And in some cases in the contemporary world, this reaction could be precisely what we require. If a thug pulls a knife on you, then this is going to provide you the ideal opportunity of fleeing to live one more day.

Chronic Stress

However, the issue comes when the danger isn't a tangible threat and when it isn't an 'urgent' threat. We just reside in a world which we didn't evolve for and this implies that a lot of our systems are basically outdated.

For instance, if you're delivering a speech, at that point, your body is going to respond in just the exact same way as it would if you discovered a forest fire. And in this instance, none of the modifications would assist at all. You'd be more prone to stuttering, you'd appear sweaty and your voice could even change.

And if you panic (in some cases stress can seem like a heart issue) then this could at some point develop a bad cycle inducing you to get more and more stressed, ultimately hyperventilating and losing consciousness as a result. This is what occurs when it comes to an anxiety attack!

Moreover, this is likewise how we react to owing money, or despising our jobs.

But we can't flee from these issues and we can't combat them. And this then implies that the fight or flight reaction can continue at 'low degree' for a long period of time. This is what we refer to as chronic stress and it's awful for all *sorts* of reasons.

For starters, chronic stress implies that our immunity and the digestive system are subdued for extended time periods. This could lead to malabsorption as we end up being less able to absorb extra nutrients from our food. And it could stop us from resting and make us more prone to the disease.

What's more, is that ultimately, this stress could induce us to 'run out' of the catecholamine neurotransmitters which make it possible for us to concentrate. This is referred to as 'adrenal fatigue,' and it's related to chronic anxiety and depression.

Note at the same time that no neurotransmitter and no hormones operate in a vacuum. If you boost one, you change others. And when you raise cortisol (connected with chronic stress particularly), you also raise ghrelin-- the appetite hormone. This likewise promotes something referred to as 'lipogenesis' implying that more of the fuel sources in your diet are going to be kept as fat rather than utilized for energy.

As a matter of fact, cortisol even breaks down muscle by creating something referred to as myostatin that tells the body to break down muscle for energy. So it's vital for your physique at the same time that you find out how not to feel stressed out when it isn't beneficial.

This is why it's so vital that we find out how to react suitably to the scenario at hand and to subdue stress when it isn't suitable, so that we could proceed appreciating life and remaining healthy. Mindfulness is the road to that.

Positive Stress

But the thing is, there is something such as 'positive stress.' The goal here is not to entirely get rid of stress from your life. Instead, it is simply to manage it.

As we've already observed, stress is a beneficial tool if you're attempting to improve your physical functionality. If you're in a race, or if you're surfing, at that point this reaction is precisely what you require to things accomplished.

But the perfect scenario would be that you obtain all the perks of the fight or flight reaction, without the downsides. Picture if you could acquire that concentration and that improved muscle mass but in the absence of the feeling of fear and dread.

As it occurs, just such a state might exist. This is what psychologists refer to as a 'flow state,' and it has a tendency to be set off during times where we are extremely concentrated on something which we also really enjoy. The example provided frequently is extreme sports, where several athletes illustrate the world appearing to slow down around them whilst they carry out incredible moves and feel more vigorous than they ever have been before.

We likewise encounter flow when we're entirely concentrated on the work we're performing, or when we're so deep in focus that we neglect the time. Throughout this state, we create identical hormones and neurotransmitters but with the inclusion of an additional one referred to as 'anandamide'-- the bliss hormone which is also linked to complex and imaginative thinking. It's really the identical chemical that offers marijuana its impact but what the majority of people don't know is that it's likewise created organically by the brain.

Keep in mind though that again this isn't truly just 'one state' but instead a spectrum. We could be somewhat stressed and really stressed. We could be somewhat alert or really alert. We could be vigilant and upset, vigilant and joyful or vigilant and scared. It's helpful to think about the brain with regards to 'states' but just understand that there are numerous states in between at the same time and it's more probable that you're someplace here on the spectrum.

Flow states aid us to operate at our finest and concentrate more, but they don't induce the identical adverse effects as a common fight or flight. The difference? Satisfaction. So if you are able to attempt and delve into the satisfaction of what you're doing and see it as an enjoyable challenge as opposed to something awful, then you're more probable to enter that flow. Locate the fun in what you're carrying out, find what you're enthusiastic about in it and find out how to really enjoy it. You should do all this utilizing very comparable techniques to the cognitive restructuring we've already noticed.

And also, you likewise require a low level of 'eustress.' Eustress is the twin of chronic stress but is once again a more desirable type. Eustress is the type of stress which encourages us to do things. For instance, if you have a test turning up and you don't experience any stress whatsoever, then there is a likelihood that you won't study for it and therefore, you won't get great marks.

Having just the appropriate degree of low level 'stress' is what you require to ensure you begin studying early and perform the best you are able to. Eustress doesn't simply have to suggest a negative inspiration. It can also suggest a positive inspiration. It's stress, but it's centered around something favorable.

Delving Into Hidden Powers

Then there's the kind of stress that can uncover additional physical and psychological potential. I'm not stating that anybody is going to manage to practice themselves to the point where they can gain access to this potential; all I'm stating is that it is real which is extremely intriguing and hopefully details the opportunities that are present and the reason why gaining access to more of your brain and your feelings is so extremely powerful.

So keeping that in mind, the first instance is a little something called a 'flashbulb memory.' This shows the potential we have to remember things in vibrant detail if we believe the event is crucial enough. Reflect on where you were at the moment you first became aware of the 9/11 attacks, or maybe where you were the moment you initially found out about Michael Jackson. Additionally, think about a moment which was especially crucial in your own life-- for bad or for good.

The odds are that you are able to recall these events in much more precise detail than you could other aspects of your biographical memory. This is what's referred to as a 'flashbulb memory.' To some extent, this is the result of continued rehearsing: when something significant takes place, we replay it again and again and again in our heads. But it's likewise the outcome of neurotransmitters being discharged that adjust how the memory is set and make those links substantially stronger.

And then there's crisis strength. Crisis strength, also referred to as hysterical strength, is the title provided to occurrences where folks instantly take advantage of amazing strength. The traditional instance here is the Mom who manages to lift a car off of their stuck child beneath. How is this achievable?

Although there is extremely little in the way of scientific research examining this phenomenon, there is an actual theory regarding how it could work.

Whenever you contract your muscle typically to lift a thing, your brain transmits signals that journey via your central nervous system and to the 'neuromuscular junction.' Acetylcholine (indeed, the neurotransmitter) is unleashed and this induces muscle fibers to fire. Only we're never very able to recruit 100% of those muscle fibers. Typically, we recruit approximately 30% of them and even a qualified athlete is going to just manage to get up to approximately 50%.

This is believed to be an evolutionary restriction, the concept being that employing 100% of our muscle would leave us totally drained and prone to attack. Furthermore, it could, in fact, result in injury by putting excessive pressure on our joints and connective tissues.

But to display the type of strength we really have hidden away, just view anybody who receives an electrical shock and gets tossed across the room. This is induced not by the electricity itself but by the person's muscles when they powerfully contract as the reaction to the shock. This induces them to gain access to 100% of their muscle fiber that is sufficient to catapult them all over the room, although they aren't utilizing a jumping technique!

And there's another way we appear to be able to take advantage of increased muscle contraction: by promoting the production of the catecholamine neurotransmitters and fight or flight hormones. It is assumed that under times of extreme stress, we could engage a lot more muscle mass and thus achieve supernatural strength.

And once again this is a range. Really, causing even a small fight or flight reaction is sufficient to somewhat boost your gym strength. Studies reveal that if we train with loud noises in the background, or if we train while clamoring (which likewise promotes the production of comparable hormones) we are really capable of involving additional muscle.

So psyching yourself up prior to a workout just could be among the ideal methods to boost your functionality in the gym! Managing, not subduing stress may just be the trick to discovering your full potential.

Chapter 6: Why You Should Consider Visualizing

Up until now, we've considered utilizing cognitive restructuring and meditation to alter our mental states. But really, it could be the case that visualization is much more beneficial and even more crucial.

The majority of folks think that we think in 'thoughts.' That is to say that we come with an internal monologue which operates like the thought boxes in comics. More recent research, however, proposes that we can think in a great deal of techniques:

In some cases we visualize, in some cases, we picture our bodies doing a thing and nearly feeling what we're thinking and occasionally we just 'know.' This latter instance is referred to as 'unsymbolized thought.'

And as a matter of fact, thinking with our senses and our bodies could just be what allowed us to create thought to begin with.

Embodied Cognition

Shortly, embodied cognition is the concept that all our thoughts ultimately connect back to physical experience.

When somebody claims something to you, or when you consider anything, your brain translates this in such a manner that provides it meaning. You don't naturally recognize the language, which indicates the brain must be 'converting' it into some type of pure meaning.

Psychologists at one time believed that the brain had a language of its own that they referred to as 'mentalese.' More recently, though, a growing number of specialists embraced the belief that we comprehend things by visualizing them. When somebody shares with you a story, you comprehend the story since your brain visualizes it occurring to you.

When somebody tells you they went through the snow, you imagine the color white, you picture the cool air on your skin and you nearly hear the noise of the crunching snow underfoot. When we consider 'higher level' thoughts, we comprehend them just because we are able to associate them back to bodily experiences abstraction. Math, besides, is essentially built upon counting.

This is likewise persistent with the idea that regions of our brain illuminate during visualization as if we were actually engaging in the activity. If you think of swinging a golf club, then neurons associated with that movement are going to activate in your brain. And as far as your mind and body are involved, that could as well be taking place!

So it makes a bunch of sense to integrate visualization with your meditation practice and with your restructuring. Don't think that visualization can 'trick' your mind into believing something is occurring and thereby change your mood? Then just attempt replaying your most distressing moments, or thinking of scenes from a really sad movie. You'll begin to feel exceptionally sad in a snap.

Visualization

One technique to utilize this power of visualization which is well recognized, is to visit a 'happy place' throughout the meditation. If you can't practice meditation in a quiet and lovely environment, then at the very least you could replicate it in your mind's eye by picturing you're on a stunning beach, in a cabin in the mountains, or in a sizable field receiving a lot of sun. But you could likewise utilize visualization so as to change your mood in other ways.

For instance, if you're having a hard time concentrating on your work, then you may use visualization to produce a little eustress to inspire you. To accomplish this, you just have to recall why you're performing the work and why it's significant to you.

Let's suggest that you're working towards a demonstration for a meeting. Visualize just how fantastic it would feel to dominate that demonstration and knock it out the park. Then visualize how doing that continuously could someday result in a better career and a better salary, for example. Now visualize the reverse: picture it going wrong and recall why it matters.

You may do the identical thing with nearly anything you're having a hard time to focusing on. By connecting what you're doing back to the psychological hook and the main reason you're making it happen, you can a lot more successfully find the dedication and drive you require to accomplish it. Maintain your goals in mind, and you are going to be inspired each day to wake up and begin exercising, or to focus on your private project, or to put in your greatest performance at work.

Chapter 7: Why is Belief so Powerful?

What a bunch of folks are going to wish to utilize these tools for is to enhance their self-esteem and self-confidence.

This is one reason we're frequently informed to visualize ourselves hitting our goals. Whenever you visualize yourself attaining a goal, you generate neurotransmitters and hormones as if you had accomplished that goal. As far as your brain is involved, that has already transpired. This then makes you a lot more probable to execute well when you, in fact, try that thing.

Also though, when we inadvertently visualize ourselves falling, or bumbling up on stage, this, in fact, causes us to create more fight or flight hormones that therefore makes us worried and makes us a lot more probable to in fact do those things.

So don't simply reorganize your thoughts, attempt to visualize things working out, and with the support of your cognitive restructuring you ought to know that this is really what's more *probable* to transpire.

Becoming Socially Fearless

Generally, eliminating anxiety and boosting our confidence is a really crucial tool, and the more you could acknowledge the power of just relying on your own capability, the more things are going to begin to go your way.

An additional tool you could utilize to get rid of social anxiety totally is hypothesis testing. The majority of us have *some* social anxiety whether or not we're usually confident, and by getting rid of this, we could end up being way more successful.

Let's begin by inquiring why confidence matters to begin with. The straightforward response is that when you're self-confident, others assume they ought to likewise be confident in you. This transmits the evolutionary indicator that you have to be higher in the pecking order, it makes the opposite sex believe that you have to be a catch and it makes the identical sex believe that you have to be a significant and prominent figure.

But whenever we stutter and bumble, it proposes that we aren't self-assured in either the material which we're explaining, or our own significance. In either case, this then makes individuals less probable to trust us, and it makes them believe that if we're reluctant of them, they have to be superior to us. The pecking order has now set us in a lot weaker place. It doesn't indicate they'll be vicious, it just indicates that we're not in a place of power and impact.

Utilizing hypothesis testing however, it's achievable to go one step further and to entirely change the manner in which individuals think of you and the means by which you interact with others.

To accomplish this, you're just going to eliminate the anxiety you formerly had when talking to folks by evaluating the result of it going wrong. So locate a store that you don't typically shop in and afterward go up to the counter to purchase something. The moment you do, do this applying a funny voice, say something intentionally unpleasant, or remain in silence for a second.

It is going to be uncomfortable and painful, and it is going to activate your fight or flight reaction. However, breathe and make an effort not to get too nervous. What you'll discover is that nothing negative comes of this experiment and the purchase is finished as usual.

That was the worst-case circumstance, and nothing horrible took place! Do this a little bit more and gradually, the reassociation is going to also begin and you'll discover that there's truly nothing to be scared of. Ultimately, things like job interviews, dates and other social situations are going to be far less intimidating and are going to induce much less of a stress reaction. The outcome? You'll seem so self-assured and comfortable, that your charisma and impact are going to improve drastically.

The Law of Attraction

But even in the absence of this action, simply engaging in mindfulness and mastering distancing yourself from your thought and feelings will aid you in becoming calmer and more self-assured. And it is going to likewise enable you to separate from adverse emotions and to, therefore, increase your self-value. There are also kinds of meditation which entail meditating on the matters you enjoy about yourself.

However you attain it, boosting your self-worth and self-confidence could ultimately start to make all sorts of things take place in your life. This is known as 'the law of attraction,' and it just suggests that whenever you believe yourself to be one particular way, you end up being like that.

So whenever you consider yourself as a highly prosperous high flyer who is going to certainly be rich someday, that's how others are going to regard you and that's the way you'll behave. You'll introduce yourself as somebody more self-assured, you'll tackle jobs with additional responsibility and you'll also dress the part. And when others think about you like that and you begin grabbing more chances for promotions, then you'll begin to really ascend the ladder.

Conclusion

We've addressed a whule lot within this guide but, ideally, you now recognize that mindfulness is a lot more than simply a potent form of meditation. Certainly, it is that also, but beyond this mindfulness simply indicates being more familiar with your own thoughts, your own body and your own views and visualizations. Whenever we accomplish this, it enables us to choose how we wish to feel, how we intend to act and what we would like to think. Rather than allowing the body and mind be reactive to our environment, we rather learn to second-guess ourselves and to ensure we are in the ideal attainable mindset and mood for the current situation.

That could mean being more vigilant so we could concentrate on work. It may imply being calmer for our wellness and for our social connections. It may indicate being more inspired for the gym. Or it could just mean being a little kinder to ourselves or altering how we speak.

Mindfulness is the trick to uncovering the complete potential of your mind and body. And whenever you could accomplish that, all sorts of doors begin to open for you.

Thank you for reading through this book and I hope that you have found it useful. If you want to share your thoughts on this book, you can do so by leaving a review on the Amazon page. Have a great rest of the day.

Printed in Great Britain
by Amazon